The United Kingd

Reading motivation and engagement in the primary school classroom: theory, research and practice

By Sarah P. McGeown

Minibook 38

UKLA Minibook Series

Series Editor Rachael Levy
Past Editors Eve Bearne, Alison B. Littlefair, Bobbie Neate, Ros Fisher, Susan Ellis

Minibooks in print

Issue number 38

Reading motivation and engagement in the primary school classroom: theory, research and practice Sarah P. McGeown

Published 2013 • ISBN 978-1-897638-71-2 • ISSN 2041-935 X

Published by UKLA © *United Kingdom Literacy Association 2013*
United Kingdom Literacy Association, University of Leicester, University Road, Leicester LE1 7RH **www.ukla.org**

Reading motivation and engagement in the primary school classroom: theory, research and practice

Contents

continues over

Contents *continued*

Chapter 1

What is reading motivation and why is it important?

Introduction

Being able to read is important, not only for academic success, but as a general life skill that is necessary in a literate society. Therefore identifying ways to improve children's reading through engagement in reading activities is crucial. Within the research field, there has been more focus on the development of cognitive (e.g., language, decoding) skills to support and improve children's reading rather than a focus on enhancing motivation to read. However, researchers are increasingly recognising that children's motivation to read is important for their reading development.

Over the past three years, colleagues and I within the Department of Psychology at the University of Hull (and now within the School of Education at the University of Edinburgh) have been researching children's reading, with a specific focus on the relative importance of cognitive and motivational factors for reading, but also investigating whether reading motivation may be more important for some groups of readers than others. The purpose of this minibook is to support teachers in fostering motivation for reading, through reference to up to date research in the field. By promoting motivation for reading, we almost exclusively refer to encouraging motivation to read books, as book reading is more closely associated with reading skill compared to other types of text (Anderson *et al.*, 1988; Clark, 2011; Spear-Swerling *et al.*, 2010). In addition, the book focuses primarily on the later years of primary school education; however practical suggestions provided are relevant for the whole primary age range.

Overview

Chapter 1 considers how motivation to read is commonly understood and defined, by looking at different theories of reading motivation. In addition, suitable assessments to measure children's motivation to read are described. This chapter concludes with a discussion about why reading motivation is important and what impact it has on children's reading skills.

Chapter 2 discusses the evidence concerning gender differences in reading motivation, differences between high and low attaining readers, and age related changes in children's motivation to read. After each of these three sections, practical suggestions are provided to target reading motivation interventions most effectively.

Chapter 3 offers practical suggestions for teachers to improve children's motivation to read within the primary school classroom. These suggestions are taken from theories of reading motivation, questionnaires and interviews carried out with teachers and children, published results from research studies, focus groups with children, discussions with teachers and school observations.

Chapter 4 provides a short summary, some concluding points and highlights the importance of integrating research and practice.

Skill and will

As reading is an effortful and purposeful activity that often involves choice and perseverance, motivation is crucial for children to develop their reading skills. In fact, there is a vast literature illustrating that children's motivation to read is related to their reading attainment (e.g., Morgan & Fuchs, 2007; Wang & Guthrie, 2004). Furthermore, research illustrates that it is not only children's cognitive skills (e.g., language, decoding skills) that are important for their reading attainment, children's motivation to read is additionally important after taking into account these cognitive abilities (Anmarkrud & Braten, 2009; Logan *et al.*, 2011; Medford & McGeown, 2011; Taboada *et al.*, 2009). In other words, to become successful readers, children need the 'skill' and the 'will'.

Theories of reading motivation

Two main theories which have been proposed to explain why children are motivated to read are the intrinsic-extrinsic theory of reading motivation and the expectancy-value theory of reading motivation.

Intrinsic and extrinsic reading motivation

The intrinsic-extrinsic theory differentiates between internal and external reasons to explain why children read. For example, if a child chooses to read because they find reading inherently interesting or enjoyable, this is regarded as an internal reason (commonly known as intrinsic motivation). However, if a child reads to get better grades or to gain recognition or praise from their parents, then this is regarded as an external reason (commonly known as extrinsic motivation).

Intrinsic reading motivation	*Extrinsic reading motivation*
Curiosity A child's desire to learn more or new things through reading	**Competition** A child's desire to outperform others in reading
Involvement A child's level of engagement or involvement when reading	**Recognition** A child's desire for their reading achievements to be recognised by others
Preference for challenge A child's desire to work with or master complex reading materials	**Grades** A child's desire to achieve good marks in reading
	Compliance A child's conformity to an external requirement to read
	Social A child's engagement in social interactions involving books and/or reading

Figure 1 Intrinsic and extrinsic dimensions of reading motivation, (adapted from Wang & Guthrie, 2004)

The eight dimensions of reading motivation proposed above provide quite different reasons or explanations about why children are motivated to read. Teachers interested in studying children's motivation to read from this perspective can use the Motivation to Read Questionnaire (MRQ) (see Wigfield & Guthrie, 1997 and Wang & Guthrie, 2004 for two different versions). The MRQ has a number of questions to measure each dimension of motivation. Examples of statements that children are asked to agree or disagree with are:

I like to read about new things

If a book is interesting I don't care how hard it is to read

I like to get compliments for my reading

I like to read to improve my grades

These four examples measure the constructs of curiosity, challenge, recognition and grades respectively.

In general, children's intrinsic reading motivation is positively associated with their reading skills (e.g., McGeown *et al.*, 2012b; Wang & Guthrie, 2004). Therefore, children with better reading skills are typically more intrinsically motivated to read (or alternatively, children who are more intrinsically motivated to read generally have better reading skills). On the other hand, children's extrinsic reading motivation is generally unrelated to their reading skills (Logan & Medford, 2011) or negatively associated with their reading skills (Becker *et al.*, 2010; Mucherah & Yoder, 2008; Wang & Guthrie, 2004).

This difference between intrinsic and extrinsic motivation has led some to conclude that fostering intrinsic reading motivation is particularly beneficial for children's reading. It is thought that children who are intrinsically motivated to read (e.g., are reading out of curiosity to learn more, or out of a desire to develop their reading skills) will be more engaged in what they are reading. As a result, intrinsically motivated children will gain a richer or deeper understanding of what they have read.

On the other hand, children who are extrinsically motivated (e.g., are reading to get a better grade or to receive recognition from their parents) are commonly thought to read with very little interest or engagement in what they are reading, and as a result, will acquire a surface level of understanding. However, it is important to recognise that children can be motivated to read for numerous reasons, both intrinsic and extrinsic. It appears to be the case that extrinsic reading motivation is not necessarily detrimental to children's reading attainment or the development of their reading skills, if it is coupled with high levels of intrinsic motivation (Park, 2011). In fact, among very good readers with high levels of intrinsic reading motivation, being additionally extrinsically motivated may be beneficial to their reading (McGeown *et al.*, 2012b).

Nevertheless, it is generally considered that intrinsic motivation is more advantageous to children's reading development; as a result a focus on developing intrinsic aspects of motivation in the classroom may be more likely to confer advantages on reading skill and engagement in literacy activities. Therefore throughout this minibook I will primarily suggest ways to develop intrinsic motivation, although I will also offer suggestions to develop extrinsic motivation.

Intrinsic and extrinsic motivation: from theory to practice

The intrinsic-extrinsic theory sets out clear suggestions for the classroom to develop children's reading motivation. For example, to foster intrinsic reading motivation, hands-on and engaging activities could be used to introduce children to some topics, with books then being provided afterwards for children to research these topics in more depth. Alternatively, by asking children what interests them and learning more about their individual interests, it may be possible to use their inherent curiosity about a topic (e.g., their favourite animal, sport or activity) to boost their motivation to read more on this topic.

Alternatively, very different suggestions would be provided to foster extrinsic reading motivation. For example, rewards or awards could be given to children for completing a book, writing a book report or working hard in a reading activity. On the other hand, children could be praised for their reading skills or their hard work in a reading task. These types of practices would be more likely to develop children's extrinsic reading motivation. More of a focus on practical suggestions is presented in Chapter 3.

Expectancy value theory of motivation

The second theory commonly used by researchers is the expectancy-value theory of reading motivation (Eccles *et al.*, 1983). This theory proposes two dimensions of motivation, that is, two general explanations about why children are motivated to read. The expectancy dimension suggests that children are motivated to read if they believe they are good at it and expect to do well in reading tasks. On the other hand, children who do not believe they are good readers and believe they will struggle in their reading will be less motivated to read. In other words, it is children's expectations of success (or failure) that motivates them.

The value dimension refers to valuing reading as an activity which is enjoyable, useful and important. This dimension suggests that those children who value reading as an important and enjoyable activity will be more motivated to read. Eccles *et al.*, (1993) have illustrated that expectancy and value dimensions of motivation are distinct as children have been found to differentiate between their self-concept and value beliefs. Therefore, you don't necessarily have to be a good reader to value reading; similarly you can be a good reader but not necessarily value reading as an activity.

Value	Expectancy
Valuing the activity as enjoyable, useful and important	*Expectations of success or failure*

Figure 2 Expectancy and value dimensions of reading motivation (adapted from Gambrell et al., 1996)

In general, expectancy (often used interchangeably with terms such as efficacy, competency beliefs or self-concept) is commonly associated with children's reading skill (Chapman & Tunmer, 1997; Morgan & Fuchs, 2007). Therefore, children with high expectations of success in reading are generally good readers. On the other hand, reading value has been found to be a stronger predictor of children's engagement in reading activities (Wigfield & Eccles, 2000). That is, children who value reading more typically read more outside school although they may not necessarily have better reading skills.

Teachers interested in studying children's motivation to read using the expectancy-value theory can use the Motivation to Read Profile (Gambrell *et al.*, 1996). This is a twenty item questionnaire. Examples of statements which children need to complete are:

My friends think I am....

a very good reader

a good reader

an OK reader

a poor reader

Knowing how to read well is....

not very important

sort of important

important

very important

These two examples are used to measure expectancy and value respectively.

Expectancy and value motivation: from theory to practice

Just as the intrinsic-extrinsic theory of motivation can highlight suggestions for practice, the expectancy-value theory of motivation also has implications for educational practice. For example, to foster greater value in reading, children could receive more education about the importance of reading as a skill that is not only useful for school, but as a life skill that they will rely on after they leave school. As value also ties into ideas about enjoying reading as an activity, finding ways to foster children's enjoyment of reading would also be important (this will be covered in Chapter 3). On the other hand, to foster greater expectancy, children should work at a level that is appropriate to allow them to build up confidence in reading and have greater expectations of success when reading texts. Fostering a balance between both aspects of motivation is important.

Why is reading motivation important?

It is unlikely that it is solely children's motivation to read that develops their reading skills. Rather, reading motivation influences the extent to which children engage in reading activities and their frequency of reading. In other words, the more motivated children are to read, the more they read, which then develops their reading skills (Becker *et al.*, 2010). Therefore, the relationship between reading motivation and reading skill may be explained, to some extent, by reading frequency and engagement in reading activities.

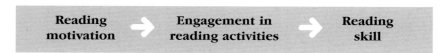

Figure 3 Indirect relationship between reading motivation and reading skill

It is not surprising that children who are more motivated to read, will read more often (Baker & Wigfield, 1999; Wigfield & Guthrie, 1997) or that children who read more often, will have better reading skills (Anderson *et al.*, 1988; Cipielewski & Stanovich, 1992; Guthrie, *et al.*, 1999). In fact, the amount of time that children spend engaging in reading activities has also been found to be a good predictor of children's growth in vocabulary, general information, spelling and language skills (Echols *et al.*, 1996).

However, reading motivation has also been found to contribute directly to reading comprehension skill, independent of its influence on children's reading frequency and breadth of reading (Wang & Guthrie, 2004). Therefore, children's reading motivation can also directly influence their reading skills.

Figure 4 Direct relationship between reading motivation and reading skill

Summary

- Both the skill (e.g., language, decoding skills) and the will (e.g., motivation to read) are important for children's reading skill and reading development.

- There are different theories of reading motivation and appropriate questionnaires which can be used by teachers to assess children's motivation to read within the primary school classroom.

- The intrinsic-extrinsic theory of reading motivation suggests children can be motivated to read because of internal reasons (e.g., a general curiosity) or external reasons (e.g., a desire for praise).

- The expectancy-value theory of reading motivation suggests that children are motivated to read because they believe they are good at it (expectancy) or because they value reading as an important, useful and enjoyable activity (value).

- Finding ways to enhance children's motivation to read is important because reading motivation is associated with children's engagement in reading activities, reading skill and reading development

Chapter 2

Individual differences in reading motivation

Whilst it is evident that children's motivation to read is generally associated with their reading attainment and engagement in reading activities, there is evidence to suggest that for some children, motivation to read may be particularly important. There are a number of factors that may explain differences among children in terms of their levels of reading motivation (e.g., the influence of parents, social or economic background factors, classroom literacy practices etc.). However, this chapter focuses only on characteristics related to the child, specifically their gender, level of reading attainment and age. It is important to understand that there are broad differences among children in terms of their levels of reading motivation and the relationship between their reading motivation and reading skill. By having this information, it may be easier to identify children who may be at greater risk of low reading motivation and therefore in need of additional support.

Gender differences

There is considerable research illustrating that girls generally outperform boys in assessments of reading attainment (Mullis *et al.*, 2007; Ming-Chui & McBride-Chang, 2006), however there is considerable overlap in the reading attainment levels of boys and girls, and many boys also outperform girls. Nevertheless, due to boys' reported underachievement in reading, researchers are interested in why these differences exist, to identify ways to reduce the gap and boost boys' reading skills (Moss, 2000; 2011). This has led to interest in the role of motivation, as boys have poorer reading motivation and reading attitudes and are less likely to read for pleasure in comparison with girls (Baker & Wigfield, 1999; Coles & Hall, 2002; Clark & Burke, 2012; Logan & Johnston, 2009; McKenna *et al.*, 1995; National Literacy Trust, 2012).

Clearly it is important that both boys and girls enjoy reading and are motivated to spend time engaging in reading activities. However, there is some research to suggest that reading motivation may be particularly important for boys. For example, it has been found that boys' motivation to read is more closely associated with their reading skills compared to girls (Logan & Medford, 2011). Similarly Logan and Johnston (2009) found that whilst boys' attitudes to reading were significantly related to their reading skill, girls' attitudes were not. In addition, Oakhill and Petrides (2007) found that boys' performance in SATs reading tests was more closely related to their level of interest in the passage topic compared to girls. These studies collectively suggest that boys' reading motivation, attitudes and interest are more closely associated with their reading skill.

Therefore it may be that boys, to a greater extent than girls, need to be successful at reading in order to be motivated and have positive attitudes towards reading. This would suggest that boys' level of reading attainment may have a greater influence on their motivation to read. Therefore boys with low levels of attainment may be more likely than girls to become disengaged or de-motivated as a result of their negative reading experiences.

However, an alternative explanation may be that boys' motivation, attitudes or interest plays a more significant role in the effort they put into reading. This suggests that if boys are unmotivated or uninterested, they are less likely to put effort into their reading compared to girls (even if girls are similarly unmotivated or uninterested). This is consistent with Williams *et al.*, (2002) who found that both boys and girls felt that girls are more inclined to put effort into work even if it is tedious, whereas boys need to enjoy the task in order to work hard. Similarly, Ainley *et al.*, (2002) found that girls were more likely than boys to persist with a text that was of lower topic interest, suggesting that their interest level does not influence their effort level to the same extent as boys.

There is also concern about lower levels of reading motivation among boys because it is well established that motivation to read is associated with increased engagement in reading activities (Baker & Wigfield, 1999; Becker *et al.*, 2010; Guthrie, *et al.*, 1999; Wang & Guthrie, 2004; Wigfield & Guthrie, 1997). Indeed girls, on average, report greater engagement in a variety of reading activities, than boys (Bosacki *et al.*, 2009; Clark, 2011; Clark & Burke, 2012; Coles & Hall, 2002; Hall & Coles, 1999; Merisuo-Storm, 2006,). However, whilst boys do report less reading for pleasure, there are some literacy activities that boys more frequently engage in, such as reading newspapers, comics and manuals (Clark, 2011), although these are less frequently recognised by children as reading activities, when compared to book reading (Clark, 2011).

Gender differences: suggestions for practice

In terms of the implications of these results for educational practice, Logan and Medford (2011) suggest that reading interventions that are attainment orientated, with realistic and manageable goals, may be particularly suitable for boys. As boys experience increasing levels of achievement through successfully accomplishing these goals, this may have a positive impact on their motivation. However, if boys' motivation plays a more significant role in the effort they put into reading, this would mean that finding ways to boost boys' motivation could impact in a positive way on their reading skills and performance during reading assessments. Either way, boys' motivation appears to play a particularly important role in their reading, therefore finding ways to boost boys' motivation to read is important.

Both boys and girls will benefit from increased efforts to enhance their reading motivation. However when implementing interventions aimed at doing so, gender differences in reading interests should be considered. Boys and girls generally differ in their reading interests (Bosacki *et al.*, 2009; Clark, 2011; Clark & Foster, 2005; Clark *et al.*, 2008; Coles & Hall, 2002; Hall & Coles, 1999; Merisuo-Storm, 2006), with girls typically reporting a preference for texts about romance/relationships or animals and boys reporting a preference for war/spy, crime/detective, sports related or science fiction/fantasy books (Clark & Foster, 2005). Nevertheless, there are some types of books which boys and girls equally report enjoying, i.e., adventure, comedy and horror/ghost stories (Clark & Foster, 2005). Therefore for whole class reading activities, it will be important to carefully consider gender differences in children's reading interests before selecting an appropriate book, as children's (in particular boys') level of interest in the text will influence how motivated they are to read that text. On the other hand, for smaller group literacy activities, grouping children with similar reading interests may be an appropriate way to enhance their engagement in the literacy activity. However, this may also lead to more single sex groups than mixed sex groups.

In addition, in recent research carried out (McGeown, in press; McGeown *et al.*, 2012a), children's identification with feminine traits (e.g., compassion) were more closely associated with their motivation to read than their identification with masculine traits (e.g., competitiveness). Indeed, research suggests that throughout childhood and adolescence, reading is typically perceived as a more feminine activity (Clark & Burke, 2012; Millard, 1997). The recent Boys' Reading Commission (Clark & Burke, 2012; National Literacy Trust, 2012) proposes that cultural norms exert pressure on boys who don't see reading as 'cool'. It also proposes that boys' reading interests clash with more feminine curriculum texts. In addition, the absence of male reading models and a largely female school workforce are all reported to impact on boys' perceptions of reading as being not for them.

Therefore, to boost boys' motivation to read, it will be important to diminish the view that reading is a more feminine activity. A number of suggestions to do this have been proposed (Clark & Burke, 2012). For example, there is a need to get fathers more involved in their sons' (and daughters') home reading activities. Currently, both boys and girls state that their mothers read more than their fathers at home (Clark & Burke, 2012); therefore increasing the quantity and quality of shared reading activities between fathers and their children is important (National Literacy Trust, 2007).

Within school, boys could also be asked to carry out research about a specific male author or compare the writing styles of a range of male authors. Similarly, teachers could contact male authors to come into school and talk to children about their favourite book or why they became an author (or, if this is not feasible, male students studying English Literature at University could be asked). These types of activities may help to lessen the perception that reading is a more feminine activity.

Another effective method of promoting reading among boys is to give them opportunities to let their opinions about literacy and reading engagement be heard. A recent study (Levy & Thompson, in press) examined buddy partnerships, where younger boys (aged 5-6) were paired with older boys (aged 11-12) to contribute towards an informational DVD to help teachers and parents better understand what factors influenced their reading engagement. Whilst the boys had autonomy over what to include within the DVD, suggestions were given, such as interviews about their experiences of learning to read, suggestions for texts other children might like and footage of them sharing books. Activities like this, which allow boys an opportunity to share their literacy experiences in a way they find enjoyable (e.g., using flip cameras to record their thoughts) are likely to promote greater discussion among boys about reading.

Summary

- In general, girls report higher levels of reading motivation and more positive attitudes to reading.

- Boys' motivation to read appears to be more closely associated with their reading skill.

- Despite gender differences in children's motivation to read, there is considerable overlap among boys and girls, therefore interventions aimed at increasing reading motivation should be given to all.

- When implementing activities or interventions to enhance children's motivation to read or promote greater engagement in reading activities, gender differences in reading interests should be considered.

- Interventions aimed specifically at improving boys' motivation to read should tackle the 'feminisation' of reading.

Differences in attainment

As reading skill and reading motivation are typically related, it is intuitive that high and low attaining readers should differ in their level of reading motivation, with higher attaining readers reporting greater motivation to read. However, when comparing readers of different attainment levels, the distinction between intrinsic and extrinsic motivation is particularly important.

Whilst research studies have generally found that children with high levels of intrinsic reading motivation have better reading skills (Becker *et al.*, 2010; Logan & Medford, 2011; McGeown *et al.*, 2012b; Wang & Guthrie,

2004), the relationship between children's extrinsic reading motivation and reading skill is not as consistent (Becker *et al.*, 2010; Logan & Medford, 2011; McGeown *et al.*, 2012b; Wang & Guthrie, 2004). In the few studies that have directly compared children with high and low reading attainment on their intrinsic and extrinsic motivation, these two groups have been found to differ in their intrinsic reading motivation, but not extrinsic motivation (Lau & Chan, 2003; McGeown *et al.* 2012b).

In addition, just as boys' motivation has been found to be more closely associated with their reading skill, there is some research to suggest that lower attaining readers' motivation plays a greater role in their reading skill and reading development (Logan *et al.*, 2011). When high and low attaining readers are given the same text to read, reading and understanding this text will be a much harder process for the less fluent readers. This suggests that reading motivation may be particularly important, as the lower attaining readers need to spend more time decoding unfamiliar words or working out the meaning of words or sentences.

Whilst children often have opportunities within the classroom to choose and read their own books, very often classroom reading practices are centred on the same text. Therefore it is important to recognise that low attaining readers may need to have higher levels of intrinsic motivation to persevere with these texts. Children with lower reading skills but high intrinsic reading motivation may be more inclined to persist with a difficult text due to interest in the topic or a desire to develop their abilities. On the other hand, children with low reading attainment and low intrinsic motivation may become more quickly disengaged and frustrated with the whole process, leading to poorer performance and fewer opportunities to develop their reading skills.

Indeed, intrinsic motivation could be thought to act as an energizer which affects children's effort and persistence (Taboada *et al.*, 2009) and for low attaining readers, this energizer may be particularly important. As a result, interventions aimed at increasing intrinsic reading motivation may be particularly important for lower attaining readers.

Differences in attainment: suggestions for practice

Whole class reading activities are often centred on the same text, which will be particularly challenging for lower attaining readers. These less fluent readers will need to be highly motivated to persevere with more challenging texts and are therefore at greater risk of becoming disengaged. Grouping children on the basis of their reading skills for various classroom literacy activities can be an effective method of increasing the likelihood that children will be engaged in the literacy task. If children are asked to work with a text that is too difficult (or alternatively too easy) then this will very likely impact their motivation to read the text. Another method to support differences in attainment among pupils is for the teacher to read books aloud to the children, making the text accessible to all.

From the perspective of enhancing motivation to read, having an accurate understanding of children's reading skills is important, so that when children are assigned to work in groups, they are reading texts at the appropriate level. However, children's literacy abilities will change over time (and not necessarily at the same rate). Therefore, if children are placed into specific literacy groups at the start of the school year, then these groups may need to be flexible as some children may progress at a faster rate than others. A literacy programme which groups children for literacy lessons on the basis of their attainment rather than age, will include regular assessments of children's reading to ensure they are working at the appropriate level (Success for All UK, accessed 2012).

In addition, if taking part in a whole class literacy activity where children are required to read the same book, then lower attaining children will very likely benefit from different aspects of the literacy activity/book being tailored to their abilities, or additional support from a teacher, teaching assistant or more able peer. Indeed, Topping *et al.*, (2011) illustrated that in the long term, cross age paired reading benefits the reading skills of younger pupils (tutee), but also older pupils (tutor). This large scale randomised controlled study provides convincing evidence to support the use of

paired reading in schools, particularly when older pupils with more advanced reading skills are paired with younger pupils learning to read.

Consistent with the expectancy dimension of the expectancy value theory of motivation, children are motivated to read if they believe they are good at it and expect to do well in reading tasks; if a child does not have the support in place to help them with more challenging books then such texts may be detrimental to their reading motivation.

Summary

- High and low attaining readers generally differ in their reported intrinsic reading motivation, but not extrinsic reading motivation.

- Less fluent readers' reading motivation may play a more important role in their reading skill and reading development compared to stronger readers.

- To ensure readers of all levels of attainment are motivated to read and engaged in literacy activities, books or activities should be based on a detailed knowledge of each child's reading skills and interests.

Age differences

In general, research suggests that children's reading motivation and attitudes towards reading decline as they become older. McKenna *et al.*, (1995) carried out a very large scale study with US primary school aged children and found a steady decline in children's attitudes toward reading with age. Whilst their attitudes to both recreational and academic reading became worse with age, the trend was particularly strong for academic reading. A large scale study in the UK examining reading attitudes at aged nine (Year 4) and eleven (Year 6) also found that older children, in general, had more negative attitudes to reading (Sainsbury & Schagen, 2004). Furthermore, longitudinal research, where the same children are followed up at various points over time (Kush & Watkins, 1996) found that over a three year period (grades 1 - 4), boys' and girls' recreational and academic reading attitudes dropped significantly.

In a recent study completed with 1811 primary school aged children in Years 3 to 8, it was found that both intrinsic and extrinsic reading motivation declined significantly with age, although declines were greater for extrinsic motivation than intrinsic motivation (McGeown *et al.*, not published). In this study, all children had completed the Motivation to Read Questionnaire (Wigfield & Guthrie, 1997) to assess their levels of reading motivation. Similarly, Henderlong Corpus *et al.*, (2009) carried out a large scale study with primary and early secondary school aged children and also found that intrinsic and extrinsic motivation declined within a year long period.

Interestingly, just as boys' reading motivation is more closely associated with their reading skill, McKenna *et al.* (1995) found that the strength of association between attainment and attitude to recreational reading becomes stronger with age. One possible explanation for this strengthening association between attitude and attainment could be that if children receive constant and consistent feedback from their reading experiences, this feedback will intensify over time, resulting in stronger and reinforced perceptions of reading. For example, if a child is poor at reading and their experiences of reading are continually frustrating and negative, this will eventually lead to the belief that the inevitable result of reading is frustration. A child's attitude towards reading may therefore become more and more positive or negative as a result of their continued positive or negative experiences with reading.

Therefore interventions to tackle children's reading attitudes and motivation should be put into place at an early age, to attempt to reduce the cycle of negative attitudes and motivation on attainment over time and promote a cycle of positive experiences and motivation.

Age differences: suggestions for practice

The literature relating to age related changes in children's reading motivation has important implications for the early years. Teachers working with young children should not underestimate the importance of fostering an enjoyment of reading at a young age. It is important that teachers working with younger children have a detailed knowledge of their reading skills to be able to provide texts at an appropriate level. If young children are expected to independently read texts that are too challenging, they may lose confidence, become frustrated and consequently disengage with reading. However, children should also have opportunities to develop their reading skills through encountering more complex texts. Joint book reading activities provide occasions for children to gain access to a wider range of texts, which not only helps to develop their reading skills, but also allows them to enjoy a variety range of texts.

It is also important that a range of books and other texts are available for young children, so that, like older children, they have opportunities to self-select books on topics that they are interested in. Indeed this is necessary even at a very young age. For example, Levy (2009a) found that dominant use of reading scheme materials in reception classes discourages children from attempting to read other books. This highlights that teachers need to ensure that from a very young age children have access to, and value, a wide variety of texts (see also Levy, 2009b).

As stated earlier, children's motivation to read can decline with increasing age. Therefore teachers working with older primary school aged children may face particular challenges when trying to improve reading motivation, particularly if children have fallen into a cycle whereby their negative reading experiences produce negative perceptions of reading. It may be an effective method for teachers to work with children with poor reading motivation and/ or poor reading skills and directly confront this negative cycle. That is, try to start over, selecting books that are at the appropriate level and of interest to the child so that they start to feel positive about their reading experiences.

Summary

- Children's motivation to read can decline with increasing age.

- The relationship between children's attitudes to reading and reading skill appears to become stronger with age.

- Teachers working with young pupils should not underestimate the importance of fostering reading enjoyment and the value of reading a range of texts

- Teachers working with older pupils may face challenges in improving reading motivation, particularly among lower attaining readers. Directly confronting the negative cycle between reading experiences and motivation may be an effective way to improve motivation to read.

Chapter 3

Boosting reading motivation: suggestions for the classroom

The aim of this chapter is to bring together findings from a variety of research methods (questionnaires, interviews, interventions, experimental studies, child-led focus groups, teacher discussions and school observations) which illustrate a range of ways to improve children's motivation to read.

Implications of reading motivation theory on practice

Chapter 1 covered two of the main theories of reading motivation: Intrinsic-extrinsic and expectancy-value theories of reading motivation. Both of these theories make predictions about the types of activities that can be created within the classroom to boost children's reading motivation. As the suggestions in this section are linked only to these theories, more suggestions for motivating readers are included later in the chapter.

Fostering intrinsic reading motivation

Some potential strategies to foster greater intrinsic motivation may be:

To promote curiosity: introduce new ideas and topics to children that are likely to be interesting and engaging and then allow them the opportunity to read more about these topics. Alternatively, hands-on engaging activities could be used to promote curiosity in a topic, with books or short texts which then allow children to find out more about the topic.

To promote involvement: create situations where children become more involved in the texts that they read, possibly through suggesting to children that they imagine they are the main character in the book or asking children to engage in role-play and act out episodes from the book.

To promote challenge: allow children the opportunity to master more difficult texts (if they wish to) and encourage children to develop their reading skills through the use of more challenging texts, but with support when needed. Paired reading/peer assisted learning may also be appropriate, to allow lower attaining readers the opportunity to read more challenging texts.

Fostering extrinsic reading motivation

Research is inconclusive with regard to the relationship between extrinsic reading motivation and reading skill. However, teachers should not ignore the potential advantages of boosting some aspects of extrinsic motivation, as long as it is not at the expense of children's intrinsic reading motivation.

To promote competition: set up opportunities for children to compete with each other in different reading related activities, for example, a competition to write the best short story, or to create the best ending to a particular book. Or alternatively, if competition between children is not deemed appropriate, then children could compete with themselves. For example, children could aim to read a certain number of books by the same author or in the same book series. An excellent example of this is the Summer Reading Challenge (The Reading Agency, 2012), which challenges children to read six or more library books over the summer.

To promote recognition: praise children for their reading practices and reading skill; however praising effort rather than attainment may be more effective in the long term. In addition, awarding stars or points for good performance could also boost recognition of children's reading activities.

To promote social engagement: different types of social activities could be set up within the classroom, where children work collaboratively together on reading related tasks. There are a number of tasks that children could work on as a group, for example, using their shared interests to research their favourite author or a topic they are all similarly interested in. In addition, creating relaxed 'comfy areas' within the classroom or library for children to read together would be helpful so they don't perceive reading as an activity that they do when 'stuck at a desk'.

To promote the importance of grades: although theories of extrinsic reading motivation suggest that grades are important, this would need to be carefully handled in the classroom. Awarding stars and/or regularly providing grades to children based on their reading skills and/or activities may be useful for some children. However, rather than grading performance, grading improvement over time or effort may be more rewarding and effective in terms of raising motivation in the long term.

To promote compliance: since apparent compulsion to read might reduce children's reading motivation, promoting compliance could be introduced as part of a reading challenge.

In addition to the intrinsic-extrinsic theory of reading motivation, the expectancy-value theory of motivation would also make similar predictions as to how to improve different aspects of children's reading motivation.

Promoting expectancy

To promote expectations of success: teachers can foster greater positive expectancy by ensuring that children are working at a level that is appropriate for them so that they experience success in their reading activities. This does not mean that children should be led away from more challenging texts, but the majority of children's reading activities should ideally allow them opportunities to experience success, in order to foster greater motivation.

Promoting value

To promote value: children could be taught more about the importance of being able to read as a skill that will be useful to them after they leave school. As value is also related to feelings of enjoyment, activities should be centred on ensuring children have enjoyable and positive reading experiences to boost this aspect of their motivation.

Whilst many of the suggestions based on the motivational theories of intrinsic-extrinsic or expectancy-value may closely align with practices already being carried out within schools, by assessing children's motivation to read using a dimensional approach (see Chapter 1), it may be possible to identify patterns of children's motivational strengths and weaknesses and target appropriate interventions based on their individual motivational

profile. The suggestions provided above are appropriate for both younger and older children, and also for higher and lower attaining readers, as long as they are tailored appropriately.

Research literature: questionnaires and interviews

In addition to proposing suggestions from theory, research is necessary to have evidence of the effectiveness of different types of interventions. The following sections will cover the more research led rather than theory led proposals for boosting reading motivation.

In questionnaire and interview research with older primary school aged children, Gambrell (1996) found that the six main features associated with motivation to read were:

1. A teacher who is a reading model

This refers to a teacher who values reading and is enthusiastic about sharing their enjoyment of reading with their pupils. Teachers can do this by, for example, sharing with pupils their favourite book(s) when they were a child and/or their favourite book(s) as an adult. If appropriate, teachers can also relay the storyline of the book they are currently reading to their pupils; by doing so, pupils will recognise that their teacher has an ongoing interest and enthusiasm to read. Cremin *et al.*, (2009) have also highlighted the value of Reading Teachers, that is, teachers who share their reading practices, preferences and habits with their pupils, and are also more familiar with children's literature.

2. A book rich classroom environment

Children need access to a range of books in the classroom or school, so they have the opportunity to select books that they are genuinely interested in. Indeed, it is not solely access to books that is necessary, but rather access to books that are of interest and are engaging to children. In order to ensure such books are available, it is necessary to learn more about children's reading interests. In a large UK survey investigating 1200 primary teachers' knowledge of children's literature, Cremin *et al.*, (2008) found that teachers' breadth of knowledge of children's fiction is relatively limited. Therefore to learn more about what children are interested in reading, pupils could be asked about their reading interests directly, or alternatively, classrooms could have a 'drop box', where children post a book wish list or topics they would like to learn more about. In addition to books, access to a range of comics, magazines and digital texts will be popular among children. However it is important that children do not engage solely with these texts at the expense of books; a balance between both is more appropriate.

3. Opportunities to self-select books

In order to enhance children's reading motivation and engagement in reading activities, children also need to have sufficient opportunities to self-select books or other texts (e.g., magazines, comics, digital texts) that they are interested in and have the time in school to read these texts. It may be that teachers plan a short period of time each day or an extended period of time each week for children to spend reading a book they have selected.

4. Familiarity with books

As children become familiar with specific authors or book series they enjoy, they tend to become more motivated to read other books in these areas. Author or series projects are popular ways of familiarising young readers with the depth and scope of an author's work. Therefore it may be advantageous for schools to stock copies of a range of books by the same author or within the same book series. In addition, to introduce children to a wider range of authors, it may be a good idea to advertise other authors who are similar to their favourite. For example 'If you like Jacqueline Wilson you might also like…' This will also broaden children's reading habits and encourage them to read more widely.

5. Social interactions with books

Many readers, both children and adults, are often motivated to read books that have been recommended to them by a friend. Therefore creating opportunities/activities whereby children recommend books to each other may be beneficial to boost motivation and interest in reading. Children could be asked to get into the habit of writing a very short synopsis after reading a book (e.g., three reasons to read this book) which could be put inside the front cover of the book and then be used by other children when selecting books to read. Or, after children have read a specific book, their name could be put in the inside cover so that any other child interested in reading that book could ask the child more about it. Alternatively, to reflect children's interest and use of computers within school, children could also have on-line exchanges about books they enjoyed (Stone, 2011).

6. Literacy related incentive that reflect the value of reading

External incentives that are book related (e.g., giving a book or book voucher as a reward) have also been suggested to increase intrinsic reading motivation.

Research literature: interventions and experimental research studies

There are also several studies which have measured the effectiveness of programmes aimed at raising children's reading motivation against programmes which have no specific focus on promoting motivation for reading (see Guthrie *et al.*, 2004a). For example, Wigfield *et al.*, (2004) compared two different reading interventions: Concept Orientated Reading Instruction (CORI: which combines the development of reading skills with methods to foster intrinsic reading motivation) and Strategy Instruction (SI: which consists of teaching multiple reading strategies such as activating background knowledge, student questioning, searching for information etc, but does not focus on fostering intrinsic reading motivation). The CORI programme encourages intrinsic reading motivation using a range of methods such as linking hands-on activities with texts, providing the opportunity for choice of topic to study and through creating opportunities for pupils to collaborate. In this particular study, the researchers found that after a 12 week period comparing CORI and SI, only the CORI programme resulted in gains in children's intrinsic reading motivation and self-efficacy, however both programmes led to increases in reading frequency.

This result has been replicated in similar studies by these researchers. For example, Guthrie *et al.*, (2000) had previously reported increases in intrinsic motivation when CORI was compared with typical classroom instruction. In addition, Guthrie *et al.*, (2004b) reported significant gains in intrinsic reading motivation, reading skill and reading strategies in class-level analyses after using CORI versus both SI and traditional instruction.

More recently, Guthrie *et al.*, (2006) have examined the effectiveness of providing interesting tasks to pupils (i.e., hands-on activities that are relatively novel and introduce pupils to new ideas) before providing books on the topic of the tasks. They found that the number of interesting tasks that children are involved in increases their motivation to read more about these topics, and that this increase in reading motivation is then associated with an increase in reading comprehension skill.

Collectively, these studies suggest that interventions or programmes aimed at promoting intrinsic reading motivation can make a significant difference to children's levels of reading motivation, and do so to a greater extent than those programmes with no, or little focus, on fostering reading motivation.

Recent research: focus groups

In a recent study carried out (McGeown & Medford, unpublished), we created focus groups with Year 5 or 6 pupils across five primary schools in England to find out from children what they thought would make reading more fun. The focus groups were set up to allow children to have a free discussion about what they did and did not like about reading and their reasons for reading or not reading.

Focus groups: favourite reading topics

In the focus groups, children reported enjoying a range of different texts, including books, magazines, comics, newspapers and internet websites. Many children commented that they would like the opportunity to read more of these types of texts in school. As children grow up in an increasingly digital age, it may become more important to ensure that they have access to a variety of texts, both digital and printed, to better align with their out of school reading habits.

In addition, in all the schools we visited, the same authors or books emerged as popular favourites and it may be that these popular books are responsible, to some extent, for the majority of social interactions involving books. Moss and McDonald (2004) illustrated that through use of school library records, it was possible to examine the social reading habits of children. Therefore, from a child's perspective, access to up to date popular authors and book series will engage them more in reading activities at school.

Focus groups: children's ideas to make reading more fun

In order to make reading more enjoyable at school, quite a lot of children said that they would like to make more use of the school library but that the library didn't have enough of the type of books they would like to read. To resolve this, some children said that they would like to help the school to choose which books were bought for the school library. In fact, many of the children thought that improving the school library and the books available would increase their motivation to read at school.

Some children also said that they would like audio books that they could listen to whilst reading the book, to help them follow the book. Similarly, Lockwood (2008) provides an extensive list of ways to engage younger and older children in reading and one suggestion is for older children to record themselves reading their books aloud to create audio recordings for younger children in school. Indeed, creating audio recordings of more advanced texts may be a good way to allow younger children to access popular books read by older children.

Finally, quite a few children had more creative ideas about how to make reading more fun. Some children said that they would like to involve more drama in literacy lessons, with ideas such as acting out scenes from books, role play, games, and quizzes about books. Other children said it would be fun to make their own versions or interpretations of books that they have read in class (e.g., re-write books from a different perspective). In addition, a few children said that it would be fun to write their own books for other children to read.

In all of the focus groups, it was clear that children enjoyed the opportunity to give their opinions about how to make reading more fun at school. It may be that as a first step towards increasing reading motivation, it would be useful for teachers to involve children more often in discussions about reading and hear their suggestions about how to make reading more fun or enjoyable at school.

Teacher discussions and school observations

In addition to the focus groups, I (Sarah McGeown) have also talked with teachers about the types of activities they carry out in school. The following highlight some of the more common practices.

1. Be a reading role model

Teachers said that they bring in the book that they are currently reading outside of school and that they make time each week to read this in class. During this time, all the children in the class are given time to read their book of choice. In fact, research suggests that this practice, where teachers become fellow readers along with their students, can have a positive impact within the classroom (Cremin et al., 2009).

2. Researching authors

Many teachers that I spoke to were aware of their pupils' favourite books and authors and some said that they used these shared interests between pupils to get them to work together on tasks such as researching more about their favourite author. Many well-known popular authors have websites available for children to learn more about them (and their books) and children can work collaboratively on these activities.

3. Create book awards

In two of the schools which I have visited, book awards have been introduced successfully. In these schools, children are responsible for nominating their favourite book for a book award and have to provide reasons as to why their book should win. Very often the shortlisted and winning books are displayed in the school library for other children to see, in addition to a summary of the book and the reasons behind it being shortlisted or winning. However it may also be appropriate to provide book awards for a variety of books of different types or genres. For example, classes or schools could introduce the 'factual' and 'fiction' book award or the 'adventure', 'comedy' or 'crime' book award. This means that children who have a variety of reading interests will all be accommodated in the book awards and have the opportunity to nominate their favourite books for an award.

Summary

- On the basis of research evidence, there are a variety of practical suggestions for boosting children's motivation to read.

- In particular, listening to children's opinions about how to make reading more fun may be a useful initial route towards increasing their reading motivation.

Chapter 4

Conclusions

The aim of this minibook was to bring together current theory and research into reading motivation with practical suggestions that can be used within the classroom.

To summarise: Chapter 1 examined different theories of reading motivation, investigated the links between reading motivation and reading skill and looked at how reading motivation can be assessed within the classroom. Chapter 2 focused on child specific factors (i.e., gender, attainment and age) and discussed how these explain variation in children's reading motivation. This chapter also looked at the implications of these differences for practice. Chapter 3 focused on practical suggestions to boost reading motivation in the classroom, taking suggestions from reading motivation theories and the research literature (questionnaires, interviews, interventions and experimental studies). In addition, practical suggestions based on recent focus groups, teacher discussions and school observations were also discussed.

It is hoped that by combining a vast body of literature relating to children's reading motivation (and related areas) you feel more informed about this area. Whilst this minibook focuses more on child specific factors (i.e., gender, attainment and age), there are evidently other factors, such as the home literacy environment, parental attitudes, peers, and social and cultural experiences that will also influence children's motivation to read. Indeed, the focus of this book is on the school environment, however more research and strategies to involve parents in their children's reading activities will be welcomed in the future.

It is also hoped that this minibook has offered readers greater knowledge of the research literature relating to reading motivation and an understanding of how this literature relates to practice. Many teachers face a challenge when trying to improve children's reading motivation and engagement in reading activities. However one of the first steps towards improving children's motivation to read may be to understand more about reading motivation, to recognise which children may be in need of additional support and then to have a range of practical suggestions to hand which can be implemented in the classroom.

A note to teachers

As an educational researcher I am very interested in hearing from teachers about their experiences in trying to boost reading motivation in the classroom. In addition, if you have found the information within this book useful for your teaching or feel it has made you more interested in reading motivation more widely, please contact me as I would be very interested to hear from you. Email: Sarah McGeown (née Logan): **s.mcgeown@ed.ac.uk**

Unfortunately it is not possible to go into detail about each of the studies cited in this book. Therefore, if you would like to read any of the articles that I have cited in more detail, I would recommend that you contact the authors of these studies directly. We are generally very happy to send information to teachers whenever requested.

Suggestions for further reading

If you are interested in reading further, there are a number of very good books available which have practical suggestions for the primary school classroom to promote children's motivation to read and engagement in reading activities. An excellent book is by Michael Lockwood (2008) *Promoting reading for pleasure in the primary school*. This provides more practical suggestions to improve reading motivation and engagement among both younger and older primary school children and is set within the context of the UK education system.

Acknowledgements

I would like to thank HEFCE UnLtd for research funding to carry out the focus groups. Project: Reading for Fun - A Pupil Led Project to Boost Reading Motivation.

I would like to express a huge thank you to the teachers and children from the following schools that have supported and participated in my research. In particular, I would like to thank: Bellfield Primary, The Green Way Primary, Mersey Primary, Parkstone Primary, Bude Park Primary, Cavendish Primary, Chiltern Primary and Cleeve Primary, all in Hull. Many thanks also to Anne McIntosh of Bellfield Primary, for her continued support, and the pupils at Bellfield Primary for allowing me to take their photographs for this book.

Thank you also to Brenda Marshall and children from Port Regis School, Shaftesbury, Dorset for photographs and Jane Bednall, Headteacher, staff and children at Elmhurst primary school, Newham London for photographs.

Finally, I would like to thank the reviewers for their insightful comments and suggestions, Angela Robertson for reading and commenting on an earlier draft and Emma Medford for her assistance with much of this research, in addition to all others involved in these projects.

References

Ainley, M., Hillman, K., & Hidi, S. (2002) Gender and interest processes in response to literary texts: Situational and individual interest. *Learning and Instruction* 12 (4) pp. 411-428.

Anderson, R. C., Wilson, P. T. & Fielding, L. G. (1998) Growth in reading and how children spend their time outside of school. *Reading Research Quarterly*, 23 (3) pp. 285-303.

Anmarkrud, Ø., & Bråten, I. (2009) Motivation for reading comprehension. *Learning and Individual Differences*, 19 pp. 252-256.

Baker, L., & Wigfield, A. (1999) Dimensions of children's motivation for reading and their relations to reading activity and reading achievement. *Reading Research Quarterly* 34 (4) pp. 452-477.

Becker, M., McElvany, N., & Kortenbruck, M. (2010) Intrinsic and extrinsic motivation as predictors of reading literacy: A longitudinal study. *Journal of Educational Psychology*, 102 (4) pp.773-785.

Bosacki, S., Elliott, A., Bajovic, M., & Askeer, S. (2009) Preadolescents' self-concept and popular magazine preferences. *Journal of Research in Childhood Education*, 23 (3) pp. 340 - 350.

Chapman, J. W. & Tunmer, W. E. (1997) A longitudinal study of beginning reading achievement and reading self-concept. *British Journal of Educational Psychology*, 67 pp. 27-291.

Cipielewski, J., & Stanovich, K.E. (1992) Predicting growth in reading ability from children's exposure to print. *Journal of Experimental Child Psychology*, 54 pp. 74-89.

Clark, C. (2011) *Setting the Baseline. The National Literacy Trust's first annual survey into young people's reading - 2010*. London: National Literacy Trust.

Clark, C., & Foster, A. (2005) *Children's and young people's reading habits and preferences. The who, what, why, where and when*. London: National Literacy Trust.

Clark, C., Osborne, S., & Akerman, R. (2008) *Young people's self-perceptions as readers: An investigation including family, peer and school influences.* London: National Literacy Trust.

Clark, C. with Burke, D. (2012) *Boys' Reading Commission. A review of existing research to underpin the Commission.* London: National Literacy Trust.

Coles, M. & Hall, C. (2002) Gendered readings. Learning from children's reading choices. *Journal of Research in Reading*, 25 (1) pp. 96-108.

Cremin, T., Bearne, E., Mottram, M., & Goodwin, P. (2008) Primary teachers as readers. *English in Education*, 42 (1) pp. 1-16.

Cremin, T., Mottram, M., Collins, F., Powell, S., & Safford, K. (2009) Teachers as Readers: building communities of readers. *Literacy*, 43 (1) pp. 11-19.

Eccles, J. S., Adler, T. F., Futterman, R., Goff, S. B., Kaczala, C.M., Meece, J. L., & Midgley, C. (1983) Expectancies, values, and academic behaviours. In J. T. Spence (Ed.) *Achievement and achievement motivation* (pp. 75-146). San Francisco, CA: W. H. Freeman.

Eccles, J. S., Wigfield, A., Harold, R. D., & Blumenfeld, P. (1993) Age and gender differences in children's self and task perceptions during elementary school. *Child Development*, 64 pp. 830-847.

Echols, L. D., West, R. F., Stanovich, K. E., & Zehr, K. S. (1996) Using children's literacy activities to predict growth in verbal skills. A longitudinal investigation. *Journal of Educational Psychology*, 88 (2) pp. 296-304.

Gambrell, L. (1996) Creating classroom cultures that foster reading motivation. *The Reading Teacher*, 50 (1) pp. 14-25.

Gambrell, L. B., Martin Palmer, B., Codling, R. M., & Mazzoni, S. A. (1996) Assessing motivation to read. *The Reading Teacher*, 49 (7) pp. 518 - 533.

Guthrie, J. T., Wigfield, A., & Perencevich, K. C. (Eds). (2004a) *Motivating reading comprehension. Concept-Orientated Reading Instruction.* London: Lawrence Erlbaum Associates Publishers.

Guthrie, J. T., Wigfield, A., Barbosa, P., Perencevich, K. C., Taboada, A., Davis, M. H., Scafiddi, N. T., & Tonks, S. (2004b) Increasing reading comprehension and engagement through concept-orientated reading instruction. *Journal of Educational Psychology*, 93 (3) pp. 403-423.

Guthrie, J. T. Wigfield, A., Metsala, J. L. and Cox, K. E. (1999) Motivational and cognitive predictors of text comprehension and reading amount. *Scientific Studies of Reading*, 3 (3) pp. 231-256.

Guthrie, J. T., Wigfield, A., & VonSecker, C. (2000) Effects of integrated instruction on motivation and strategy use in reading. *Journal of Educational Psychology*, 92 (2) pp. 331-341.

Hall, C. & Coles, M. (1999). *Children's reading choices*. London: Routledge.

Henderlong Corpus, J. H., McClintic-Gilbert, M. S., & Hayenga, A.O. (2009) Within-year changes in children's intrinsic and extrinsic motivational orientations. Contextual predictors and academic outcomes. *Contemporary Educational Psychology*, 34 pp. 154-166.

Kush, J.C. & Watkins, M.W. (1996) Long-term stability of children's attitudes towards reading. *The Journal of Educational Research*, 89 (5) pp. 315-319.

Lau, K., & Chan, D. W. (2003) Reading strategy use and motivation among Chinese good and poor readers in Hong Kong. *Journal of Research in Reading*, 26 (2) pp. 177-190.

Levy, R. (2009a) Children's perceptions of reading and the use of reading scheme texts. *Cambridge Journal of Education*, 39 (3) pp. 361-377.

Levy, R. (2009b) 'You have to understand words... but not read them'; young children becoming readers in a digital age. *Journal of Research in Reading*, 32 (1) pp. 75-91.

Levy, R., & Thompson. (in press) Creating 'Buddy Partnerships' with 5 and 11 year old boys: a methodological approach to conducting participatory research with young children. *Journal of Early Childhood Research*.

Lockwood, M. (2008) *Promoting reading for pleasure in the primary school*. London: SAGE Publications.

Logan, S., & Johnston, R. (2009) Gender differences in reading ability and attitudes: examining where these differences lie. *Journal of Research in Reading*, 32 (2) pp. 199-214.

Logan, S., & Medford, E. (2011) Gender differences in the strength of association between motivation, competency beliefs and reading skill. *Educational Research*, 53 (1) pp. 85-94.

Logan, S., Medford, E., & Hughes, N. (2011) The importance of intrinsic motivation for high and low ability readers' reading comprehension performance. *Learning and Individual Differences*, 21 pp. 124-128.

McGeown, S. P. (in press) Sex or gender identity? Understanding children's reading choices and motivation. *Journal of Research in Reading*.

McGeown, S., Goodwin, H., Henderson, N., & Wright, P. (2012a) Gender differences in reading motivation. Does sex or gender identity provide a better account? *Journal of Research in Reading*, 35 (3) pp. 328-336.

McGeown, S. P, Norgate, R., & Warhurst, A. (2012b) Exploring intrinsic and extrinsic reading motivation among very good and very poor readers. *Educational Research*, 54 (3) pp. 209-322.

McKenna, M.C., Kear, D.J. & Ellsworth, R.A. (1995) Children's attitudes toward reading. A national survey. *Reading Research Quarterly*, 30 (4) pp. 934-956.

Medford, E., & McGeown, S. (2011) Cognitive and motivational factors for reading. The need for a domain specific approach to motivation. In *Psychology of Motivation. New Research*. (Eds. J. Franco & A. Svensgaard). Nova Science Publications.

Merisuo-Storm, T. (2006) Girls and boys like to read and write different texts. *Scandinavian Journal of Educational Research*, 50 (2) pp. 111-125.

Millard, E. (1997) Differently Literate: Gender identity and the construction of the developing reader. *Gender and Education*, 9 (1) pp. 31-48.

Ming Chiu, M., & McBride-Chang, C. (2006) Gender, context, and reading: A comparison of students in 43 countries. *Scientific Studies of Reading* 10 (4) pp. 331-62.

Morgan, P.L., & Fuchs, D. (2007) Is there a bidirectional relationship between children's reading skills and reading motivation? *Exceptional Children* 73 (2) pp. 166-83.

Moss, G. (2000) Raising boys' attainment in reading: some principles for intervention. *Reading*, 34 (3) pp. 101-106.

Moss, G. (2011) Policy and the search for explanations for the gender gap in literacy attainment. *Literacy*, 45 (3) pp. 111-118.

Moss, G., & McDonald, J. W. (2004) The borrowers: library records as unobtrusive measure of children's reading preference. *Journal of Research in Reading*, 27 (4) pp. 401-412.

Mucherah, W. & Yoder, A. (2008) Motivation for reading and middle school students' performance on standardised testing in reading. *Reading Psychology*, 29 pp. 214-235.

Mullis, I.V.S., Martin, M.O. , Kennedy, A.M. and Foy, P. (2007) *PIRLS 2006 international Report: IEA's progress in international reading literacy study in primary schools in 40 countries*. Chestnut Hill, MA: Boston College.

National Literacy Trust (2007). Getting the Blokes on Board. **www.literacy trust.org.uk/assets/0000/2298/Blokes.pdf** (Accessed 28th November, 2012.)

National Literacy Trust (2012) *Boys' Reading Commission*. **www.literacy trust.org.uk/assets/0001/4056/Boys_Commission_Report.pdf** (Accessed 28th November, 2012.)

Oakhill, J.V., & Petrides, A. (2007) Sex differences in the effects of interest on boys' and girls' reading comprehension. *British Journal of Educational Psychology* 98 pp. 223-35.

Park, Y. (2011) How motivational constructs interact to predict student's reading performance. Examples from attitudes and self-concept in reading. *Learning and Individual Differences*, 21 pp. 347-358.

Sainsbury, M. & Schagen, I. (2004) Attitudes to reading at ages nine and eleven. *Journal of Research in Reading*, 27 (4) pp. 373-386.

Spear-Swerling, L., Brucker, P.O., Alfano. M.P. (2010). Relationships between sixth-graders' reading comprehension and two different measures of print exposure. *Reading and Writing: An Interdisciplinary Journal* 23 pp. 73-96.

Stone, G. (2011) *The Digital Literacy Classroom*. Leicester: United Kingdom Literacy Association.

Success for All UK. **www.successforall.org.uk** (Accessed 28th November, 2012.)

Taboada, A., Tonks, S. M., Wigfield, A., & Guthrie, J. T. (2009) Effects of motivational and cognitive variables on reading comprehension. *Reading and Writing* 22 pp. 85-106.

The Reading Agency (2012) *Summer Reading Challenge*. **http://summer readingchallenge.org.uk** (Accessed 28th November, 2012.)

Topping, K., Miller, D., Thurston, A., McGavock, K., & Conlin, N. (2011) Peer tutoring in reading in Scotland: thinking big. *Literacy*, 45 (1) pp. 3-9

Wang, J.H., & Guthrie, J. T. (2004) Modelling the effects of intrinsic motivation, extrinsic motivation, amount of reading, and past reading achievement on text comprehension between U.S and Chinese students. *Reading Research Quarterly* 39 (2) pp. 162-186.

Wigfield, A. (1997) Reading motivation: A domain specific approach to motivation. *Educational Psychologist*, 32 (2) pp. 59-68.

Wigfield, A., & Eccles, J. S. (2000) Expectancy-value theory of achievement motivation. *Contemporary Educational Psychology*, 25 pp. 68-81.